Reading 0118
Battle 0118

KT-419-117

Exploring the
Maya
empire

World history

First Middle East civilisations: Sumerians and descendents (11000BC–1268AD)

Izamal
Chichen Itza
Mayapan
Coba
Uxmal
Tulum
Sayil Kabax
Labna
Campeche
Edzna

Altun Ha

Palenque

Piedras Negras
Tikal
BELIZE

Yaxchilan
Bonampak

MEXICO
Seibal
Lubaantun

GUATEMALA

Quirigua

Utatlan

Iximche Mixco Viejo
Copan

HONDURAS

Maya timeline

Writing and religious rituals are developed. Pyramid temples are built.
Maya develop separately from other peoples like the Olmecs.

| 10,000 BC | 3,000 BC | 200 AD |

The ancestors of the Maya arrive.   Pottery and weaving   Cities grow up. Kings rule each city. The biggest are T
Simple farming begins.   are developed.   Calakmul, Copán, Palenque, Uxmal, Cobá and Cara

Maya (3000BC–1697AD)

Aztecs (1100–1521)

WWII (1939–1945)

| 4000 BC | 3000 BC | 2000 BC | 1000 BC | 0 | 1000 AD | 2000 AD |

Ancient Greeks (800–146BC) Anglo-Saxons (450–1066)

Tudors (1485 –1603) Victorians (1837–1901)

Vikings (800–1066 /1400)

Ancient Egyptians (3000–332BC) Romans (700BC–476AD)

Contents

Look up the **bold** words in the glossary on page 32 of this book.

The Maya lived in the rainforests of Central America and southern Mexico. This map shows their main cities.

Wars break out between cities.

Rise of the Toltecs.

Rise of the Aztecs.

Last Maya city conquered by Spanish.

| 1000 | | 1500 | | 1697 |

Metal-working begins.

Many big Maya cities abandoned.

Spanish arrive and begin to destroy the Maya civilisation.

Meet the Maya

The Maya were descended from the first people to arrive in the Americas. These people came from what is now Russia, and they made their way south through America tens of thousands of years ago. These people got used to farming on the plains of North America, and their distant relatives – the people who call themselves American Indians – still do. But as some of them continued to move south, so they came across forests.

The Maya settled and grew up among these forests, in what are now southern Mexico, Guatemala, Belize and Honduras. They had to learn to cope with, and flourish in, this land – and for three thousand years they succeeded, before many of them suddenly disappeared.

Just like other **civilisations** of this early time (for example, the Sumerians of the Middle East and the ancient Egyptians) they built pyramids in stone. They had no contact with other civilisations outside America at all. It was all their own idea. It tells us that wherever people are, they tend to have the same beliefs and ways of life.

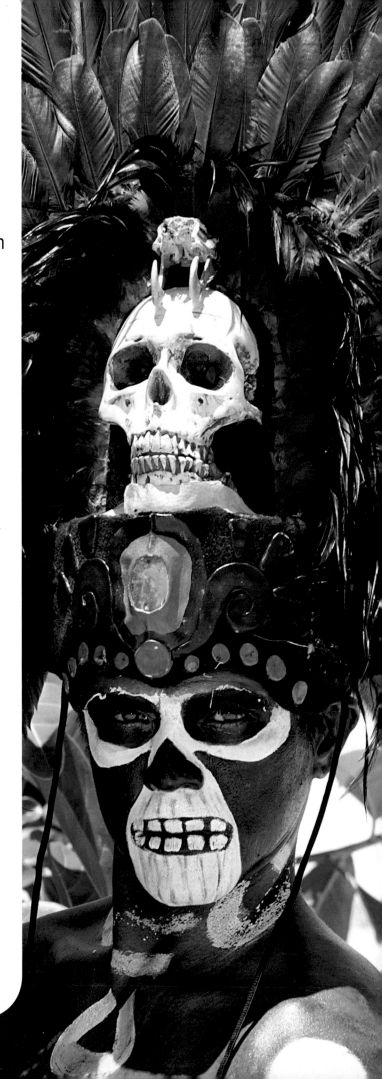

Did you know… ?

- Unlike many other old peoples, the Maya never went away. Somehow or other they survived. Now some of them reconstruct what it might have been like to be a Maya in historic times through ceremonies and events for tourists. You can see that here.

Q **Where did the Maya live?**

In their day, the Maya (and other, later, tribes in the area, such as the Aztec), were organised into powerful kingdoms, lived in huge cities, and developed empires. They invented picture writing (hieroglyphics), looked at the stars and became astronomers, and learned how to change wild plants into crops they could farm. They also learned how to **irrigate** their lands. In short, they were a people of amazing inventiveness.

It is actually surprising what we still owe to these early people. Next time you have a piece of chocolate, for example, or eat a piece of sweetcorn, you have the Maya to thank.

When the Spanish **conquistadors** arrived in the Americas in the 16th century, they destroyed many civilisations, most notably the Aztec. They tried to destroy what was left of the Maya, too, in the mistaken belief that the Maya world was inferior to the world of the Christian Spanish. But the Maya have survived. Even the Maya language has survived.

This is their story.

Most Central American empires built pyramids with shrines on top. These are Maya pyramids at Edzna.

Did you know… ?

- When the Spanish arrived all of the Maya books they could find were ordered to be destroyed by Bishop Diego de Landa in July 1562. De Landa wrote: "We found a large number of books in these characters (hieroglyphs) and, as they contained nothing in which were not to be seen as superstition and lies of the devil, we burned them all, which they (the Maya) regretted to an amazing degree, and which caused them much affliction."

Q **What are two things we owe to Maya inventiveness?**

Maya books

The Maya had a well-developed civilisation. They kept whole libraries of books containing information about their history, beliefs, astronomy and calendars. But the conquistadors and missionaries who invaded from Spain in the 16th century were not sensitive to this, and they destroyed much of this invaluable material. Only a few books survive, and you see pages from them here.

All of these pictures are pieces of what remains of the Maya books. Unfortunately, it is not very much.

Q What did the Maya use for paper?

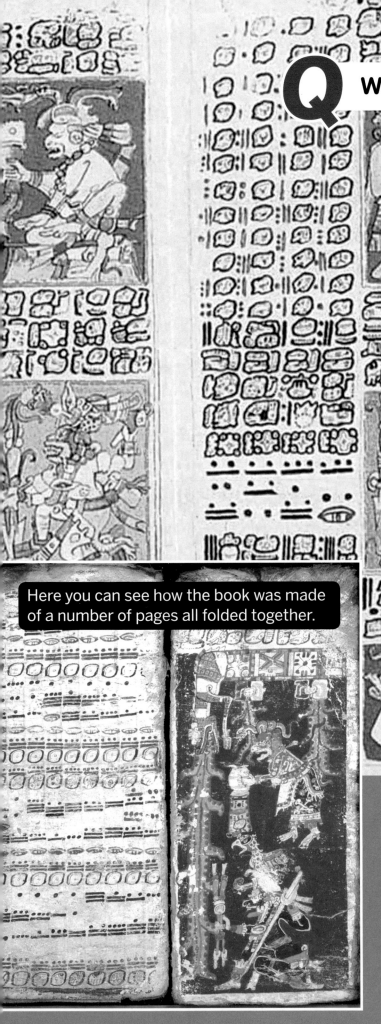

Here you can see how the book was made of a number of pages all folded together.

Did you know… ?

- A Maya book is different to books we are used to. Each book was made of a long strip of paper which was folded.
- The pages are quite large – about 12cm by 24cm. They were painted in black, red, green, brown, blue and pink, with everything outlined in black.
- The book was painted on both sides of the paper. You read along one side of the paper strip, from left to right, and then turned the book over and read the other side.
- The paper was made from the bark of fig trees. They pounded the bark fibres into a pulp with stones, and mixed in natural gums so that the pressed-out fibres would hold together. When the paper was dry, the surface was painted with white lime. The writing was done on that.
- The Maya wrote about calendars, history, gods and spirits, weather and astronomy.

Writing, counting and time

Many peoples in Central America used the same kind of calendar. The Aztec calendar, for example, looks a lot like the Maya one.

The Maya calendar is quite complicated, and is based on 260 days. They also used the 365 days of the year that we are used to. These two calendars were combined to give a 52-year 'century'.

A different calendar was used to track longer periods of time. This is called the Long Count – a count of the days since the year when they believed creation occurred (3114 BC in our calendar).

Maya did not count in tens as we do, but in twenties.

Months of the Maya calendar

Pop	Uo	Zip	Zotz
Tzec	Xul	Yaxkin	Mol
Chen	Yax	Zac	Ceh
Mac	Kankin	Muan	Pax
Kayab	Cumhu	Uayeb	

Did you know… ?

- The Maya were believers of rituals (organised ways of doing things). So they needed people to set out the rules. This was the job of the priests. The priests were in touch with the spirit world of the gods and the people.

Maya numbers

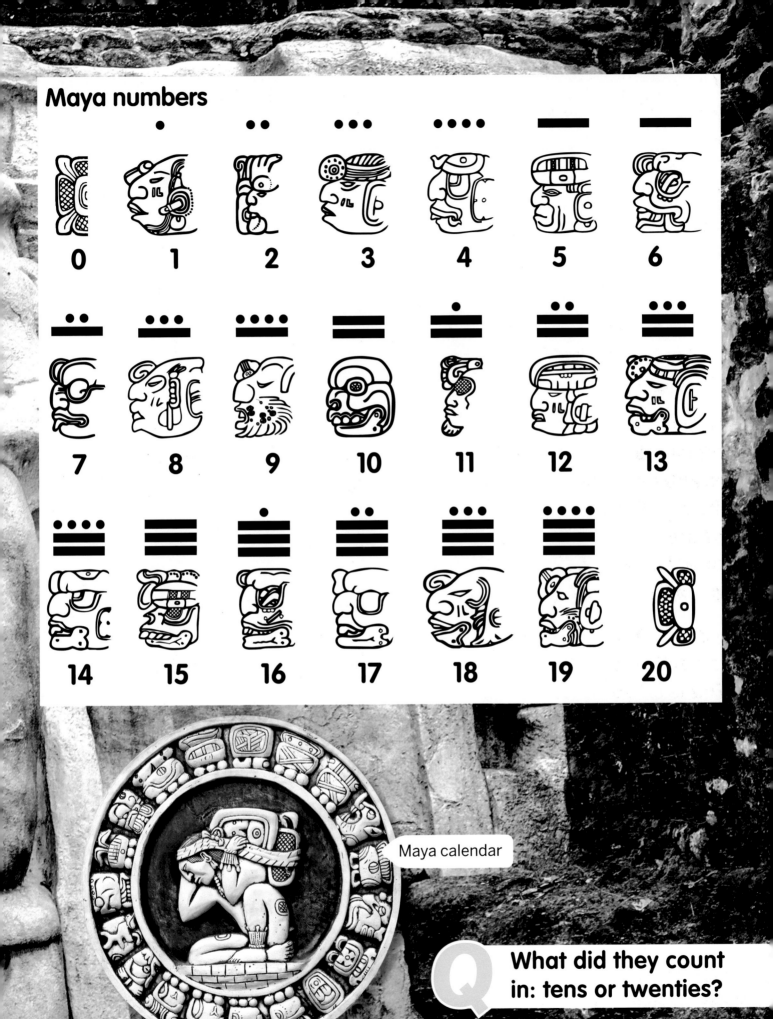

0　1　2　3　4　5　6

7　8　9　10　11　12　13

14　15　16　17　18　19　20

Maya calendar

Q **What did they count in: tens or twenties?**

Farming

The Maya lived in the rainforest and, for much of their history, they used simple stone tools. So they had to find an easy way of clearing the land. Like most other peoples in the world, they discovered that if the big trees were hacked down and left to dry during the short dry season, it was then possible to set fire to them. This is called slash and burn farming (the Maya name for it was 'milpa'). Fire got rid of everything but the tree stumps, so that a stick could be used to make holes in the soil and seeds of, for example, maize, dropped into them. The burned trees left behind an ash, which is a natural fertiliser, so the land was cleared and fertilised all in one go. The plots where they did this were little forest gardens, which they called 'pet kot'.

The problem with slash and burn farming is that the ash of burned trees soon gets used up, and the land becomes poor. It can be made to last longer by growing one kind of crop in it and then another different kind of crop. This is called crop rotation. But whatever you do, without putting fertiliser back in the soil, plants get weaker year by year. Then farmers have to cut down and burn another area.

The Maya knew that, after a few decades, new trees would grow in the old farming plots, so they could be cut down and burned again. But with lots of land out of action all the time, people needed a lot of land. If the population grows fast, a people can easily run out of good land to farm, and will either die from starvation or have to move away. And that is probably what happened to the Maya.

This is what the area of the Maya looks like today. It gives a good idea of how hard they had to work to turn it into farmland.

Did you know… ?

- The Maya understood the trees as part of the living world. The tall kapok tree, for example, was the sacred tree of the Maya.

- Some Maya lived in quite hilly land. The only way they could make use of this was by digging out level fields. This is called terracing. They made walls of stone and then dug out the soil from up the slope so that it filled the ground behind the stones.

- The other kind of land the Maya had to cope with was land that was often flooded. This occurred in valley bottoms. In order to farm this, they dug canals into the swamps and pitched the swamp mud onto the nearby land. The result was to make both drainage canals and raised beds about a metre high. The raised beds could give more crops than the other kinds of land because fish droppings in the canals made a natural fertiliser. Water lilies growing in the canals could be cut and dumped on the raised beds to make compost.

Q How did they farm in the swamplands?

13

Food from the forest

Most of the Maya were farmers. Their diet was mainly corn (maize), beans, chillies and squash – the same as the diet of the people who live there today. It is a simple, but healthy and balanced diet.

The maize seeds were ground to give flour. The Maya also made maize flour into a kind of gruel (called atol), and by adding vegetables this would have made a thicker soup, like the pottage developed in Europe at the same time. It was simply an adaptation to what was available: starch and vegetables, with the occasional piece of meat or fish thrown in when it could be caught or slaughtered.

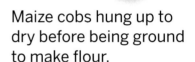

Maize cobs hung up to dry before being ground to make flour.

It is possible that it was also baked into tortillas. So Maya food would not have been unlike basic modern Mexican food. Like modern Mexicans, they added variety to this with fruits, such as avocados, and starchy root foods, such as sweet potato and cassava, both of which were easier to grow than maize.

For flavourings and drinks they had cocoa beans, vanilla beans, papaya, pumpkin and tomatoes. They also harvested cotton. All of these were cultivated from wild rainforest plants.

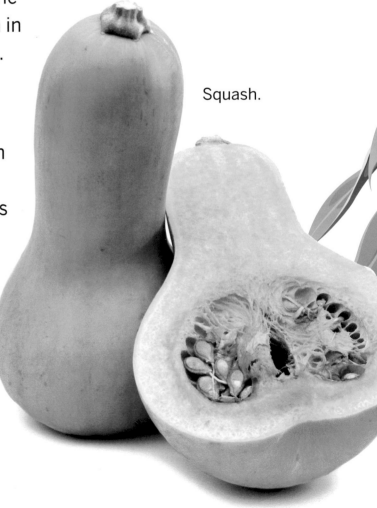

Squash.

Did you know… ?

- Turkeys are native to America. The Maya used the feathers from turkeys and ducks for clothes.
- Turkeys and ducks were also an important food. They were raised to live among the houses, just as we do today.
- The Maya were one of the first peoples to make beehives so that it was easier to collect honey.

Q **What was the Maya's main diet?**

Turkey.

Maize flour.

Cacao to chocolate

The word cacao might not be very familiar to you. But it is the tree whose beans give us chocolate. The Maya, Aztec and other Central American peoples all harvested the pods of cacao trees for their beans. You can see the pods and beans here.

To make the beans give out their flavour they have to be pulled out of their pods and fermented. This is as simple as leaving the beans in piles for a few days. Then the beans are dried and roasted.

During roasting many of the substances in the beans change, and new oils are made. These oils give the flavouring that we call chocolate.

The cacao beans were ground up and mixed with water, chilli peppers, maize and honey to make a drink called xocolat (which is where our word chocolate comes from).

Only the **nobility** could drink xocolat.

Did you know... ?

- The Maya didn't just use cacao beans as a drink. To buy cheap goods they used cacao beans as money. A small rabbit was worth 30 beans, and a turkey egg cost 3 beans.
- They used cacao beans as ceremonial sacrifices to their gods.
- They didn't know hard chocolate as we know it today. That was invented later, in Europe. They used cacao as a drink. But they did identify it as an important forest tree crop. And this is what the Spaniards saw when they began to conquer Maya lands.

Q What does the cacao plant produce?

Ripe (red) cacao pod.

Roasted cacao beans showing the skin.

Ordinary Maya homes

If you were to go to visit the ruins of Maya cities, you would find stone temples and palaces. But that is not where the vast majority of the people lived. They lived in huts made from the products of the forests, just like people the world over.

Huts made from wood, mud and thatch do not survive for long once they have been abandoned, so you have to imagine a Maya city as made up of thousands of huts like this one.

In this museum reconstruction, part of the wall has been left uncovered so that you can see it is made from saplings tied together and then plastered over with mud, dung and straw. It is remarkably similar to small huts in other parts of the ancient world, for example, Roman, Saxon or Medieval Britain. This shows how people, with the same kinds of materials (reeds, saplings and soil) make the same kinds of buildings the world over.

The floor would have been bare earth.

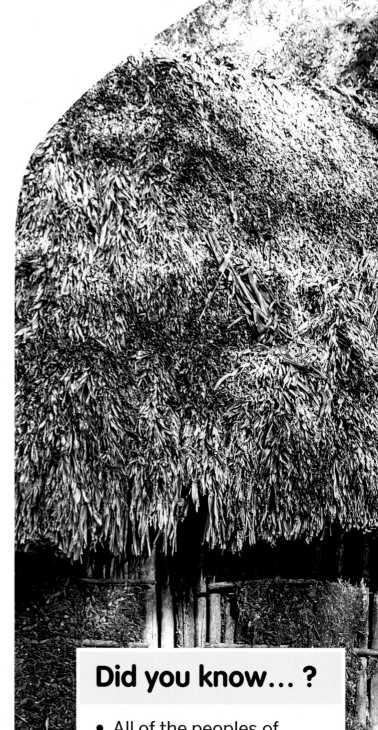

Did you know... ?

- All of the peoples of Central America shared many of the same building styles and ways of life, just as you would find similar styles all over Europe or North America. So a home built by Maya would be much the same as one built by Olmec or Aztec peoples.

The Maya cooked around a central fire, mainly making a thick soup based on maize flour. But they may also have baked flour to make tortillas, too. They were also experts at using herbs from the forest to cure illness.

Q How did the Maya build most of their homes?

Ceremonies and gods

The Maya were believers in rituals (organised ways of doing things). So they needed people to set out the rules. This was the job of the priests. The priests were in touch with the spirit world of the gods and the people.

The Maya believed in human sacrifice, just like many other societies around the world at that time, but it was not on the huge scale of the Aztecs.

Their main god was called Itzamna. Interestingly, he was the first writer and the first to develop a calendar, showing that knowledge was the most highly-regarded thing in Maya civilisation.

There were many other gods, for example a Maya maize god and the Howler Monkey Gods.

Here you see some people of Maya descent **re-enacting** what is believed to be a traditional ceremony. During Maya times the building would have been clear of all plants and the stonework would have been painted in bright colours.

Did you know… ?

- Just like monks in Medieval Europe, the Maya priests were almost the only people who could read and write. They were the keepers of knowledge, the people who wrote the calendars and much more. It is likely that the king was often regarded as the head priest as well as ruler.
- The priests used 'helper spirits'. But they were also responsible for offering sacrifices and prayers. The role of priests was passed on from father to son.
- The priests painted their skins and used tall **headdresses** of feathers set with skulls.

Q How did the priests dress?

Ballgames and myths

How did the Maya pass the time? At night they told stories, like all peoples do, and those stories got handed down as myths and legends.

In the big cities, they also played a special kind of ballgame known as pok-ta-pok. Ballcourts were built to house these games and were long, narrow alleys with ramps on both sides. The players struck the ball with their hips, keeping the ball off the ground and trying to get it through a ring. The ball was made of solid rubber 25cm across and weighed about 2kg!

The game was partly religious, and often featured human sacrifice.

This is a ballgame court. The ring was set above the middle of the Maya ballcourt. The setting sun of the equinox shone through the ring, showing how games and religion were connected.

You will find a myth story that relates creation to the ballgame on page 32.

A Maya high priest instructing scribes as drawn onto a Maya pot about 600AD. Scribes were among those who recorded myths and legends. Note the headdress and see page 30 for modern comparison.

Q What did they use in a ballgame?

Did you know… ?

- The Maya valued their ballgame above most other things, just as we value football competitions, or the Olympic Games. Games between cities were even used to settle disputes instead of going to war. However, you would not want to lose one of those important matches, for if you lost a ballgame between cities, the chances are you would become a sacrifice and have your head impaled on a stake near a temple.

Cities

Many Maya lived in cities. In the centre, people built large flat, paved areas we now call plazas, and surrounded them with palaces and temples. They connected their plazas by roads (causeways).

Most buildings were cut from stone in local quarries to save having to carry blocks far. They also used limestone as it is quite soft, and easy to cut and shape using stone tools.

There was a further bonus to this. As the rock was quarried, it left large pits. These were plastered over to make them waterproof, and used as tanks for drinking water. The main plazas were also plastered over to make them watertight, and given slight slopes so that rainwater would drain into the tanks.

Religious stages

Platforms were built about four metres high. On them there were carved sculptures, but they were also places where there were stakes on which the heads of victims or defeated ballgame players were displayed.

This picture shows carved jaguar heads beside temple steps.

Q **Why did the Maya need so many people to build pyramids?**

This picture shows a pyramid and a raised platform, or stage, with sculptures.

Palaces and temples

Palaces were large one-storey buildings. But the most striking buildings were the pyramids – raised up to put shrines as close to the heavens as possible.

The outside edges of the shrine roofs were carved with pictures of the king and could also have been seen from great distances, telling others of the power of the city.

Some pyramids were also built over the tombs of kings.

The Maya were keen astronomers, and many temples have doorways aligned with the stars. Some temples are round, and often called "observatories", although there is no real evidence for this.

Did you know... ?

- The Maya did not have metal tools, draft animals like oxen, or wheeled carts. This makes what they built all the more remarkable. So everything needed huge numbers of people to push and pull stones about.
- Much of the mortar for 'cementing' blocks together was crushed, burnt and mixed limestone. The same material was used for plastering over the stone.

The rise and fall of Maya cities

The Maya cities were vast, with tens of thousands of people living in each one. But, except where archaeologists have scraped away the rainforest to show a little of what they were like, they are almost lost as the rainforest reclaims its own. Why is this? It wasn't the Spanish. Maya cities had mainly gone centuries before the Spanish arrived.

Rise and fall of Tik'al

To find out what happened, we will look at one of the biggest cities. It is now called Tik'al or, as the Maya called it, Yax Mutal, meaning 'the first city of the kingdom of Mutal'.

This large raised platform was started about 350BC. It is made of small pyramid tombs to great kings. In front of it there are 43 stone tables telling of the successes of the kings, and 30 altars.

This pyramid is a temple to a dead king. It is the Temple of the Great Jaguar. It was built in the 8th century AD, and so is one of the last temples built before the city was deserted. The king's tomb was placed below ground level, and the temple raised over it in nine stepped levels, representing the nine levels of the underworld. The top is 47m above the Great Plaza. The roof of the shrine is decorated with stone blocks carved to represent the enormous figure of the king.

This jade carving of the king was found in the royal tomb.

Did you know… ?

- Tik'al once covered more than 16 sq km and had 3,000 buildings. The tallest temple at Tik'al rises 154m from the ground.

This is the city square, the Great Plaza.

Q **What was the main pyramid for?**

Tik'al was one of the Maya's largest cities, possibly being home to about 100,000 people. It was lived in for longer than almost anywhere else.

People began to build temples here in the 4th century BC, continuing until the 9th century AD.

These people were powerful warriors. But they were always at war. By the 9th century Maya cities like Tik'al were in crisis. They had fought so many battles their cities were exhausted. It was no longer safe to farm the outlying regions, and more and more people poured into the cities. They had to try to get more and more food from less and less land. They cut down more and more forest to get more farmland. The heavy rain eroded the now bare hillside soils.

But the cities could not find enough food for them all. As a result, the soil became exhausted until it would feed no more. The Maya had caused their own environmental disaster. So, between 830 and 950 AD, the people rebelled. They burned the

palaces of kings and nobles. Then most people fled, the cities finally fell into silence, and the rainforest claimed the ruins for the next thousand years.

Over the following centuries, people from the area used some of the stones for their own buildings, which is why many of the Maya buildings appear as ruins.

The picture below shows how just a tiny part of the city now stands above the rainforest. All the forest you now see was cleared farmland in Maya times.

So when the Spanish came, they found a people living in small villages, not huge cities. Nonetheless, they were still keen to remove traces of their amazing history (see page 7).

Did you know… ?

- Spanish conquistador Hernan Cortes passed within a few kilometres of the abandoned ruins of Tik'al but did not even know they were there because the rainforest had already hidden them.

Q **Why was the city abandoned?**

The Maya people are known for their brightly coloured fabrics. Each village has its own distinctive pattern, so you can still often tell a person's home town by looking at the pattern.

The end of Maya times?

There were important differences between how the Spanish dealt with the Maya and other empires like the Aztec. The Aztec empire was ruled by one emperor (Mochtezuma). When the Spanish conquistadors killed him, the Aztec empire fell apart.

By contrast, it took the Spanish 170 years and the loss of tens of thousands of soldiers to conquer the Maya. This was because the Maya empire was made up of many independent peoples living throughout the rainforest. None of them were friendly to the Spanish, and they fought back. The Maya lands had no gold or silver, so the Spanish had less interest in them. The final Maya were only overcome in 1697. Even then they did not lose their identity, despite the Spanish destroying almost all of their historic books.

Today the descendents of the Maya live in little villages all over the region, many still speaking the Maya languages and wearing traditional textiles.

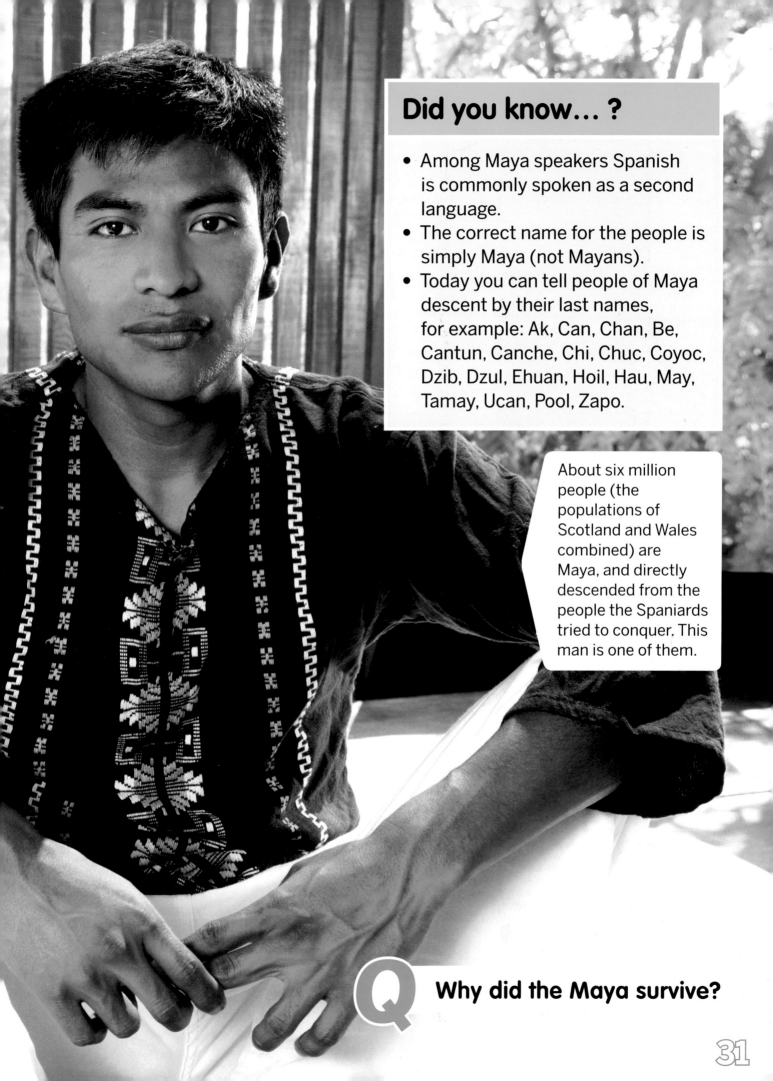

Did you know… ?

- Among Maya speakers Spanish is commonly spoken as a second language.
- The correct name for the people is simply Maya (not Mayans).
- Today you can tell people of Maya descent by their last names, for example: Ak, Can, Chan, Be, Cantun, Canche, Chi, Chuc, Coyoc, Dzib, Dzul, Ehuan, Hoil, Hau, May, Tamay, Ucan, Pool, Zapo.

About six million people (the populations of Scotland and Wales combined) are Maya, and directly descended from the people the Spaniards tried to conquer. This man is one of them.

Q **Why did the Maya survive?**

Glossary

civilisation
A people with an organised way of life and who have learned to write.

conquisadores
Soldiers of the Spanish army that invaded the Americas in the 15th and 16th centuries.

headdress
A decoration placed on top of the head.

irrigate
To water the ground during a dry spell.

nobility
People who, with the king, rule the rest of the people.

re-enact
To try to make a performance to show what might have happened in the past.

Index

Curriculum Visions

Curriculum Visions Explorers
This series provides straightforward introductions to key worlds and ideas.

You might also be interested in
Exploring the Aztec empire, Exploring ancient Egypt, Exploring ancient Greece and Exploring rainforest people.

You will find multimedia resources covering the Maya empire as well as other aspects of history, geography, religion, MFL, maths, music, spelling and more at:

www.CurriculumVisions.com

(Subscription required)

© Atlantic Europe Publishing 2014

The right of Brian Knapp to be identified as the author of this work has been asserted by him in accordance with the Copyright, Designs and Patents Act 1988.

All rights reserved. No part of this publication may be reproduced, stored in a retrieval system, or transmitted in any form or by any means, electronic, mechanical, photocopying, recording or otherwise, without prior permission of the copyright holder.

Author
Brian Knapp, BSc, PhD

Senior Designer
Adele Humphries, BA, PGCE

Editors
Gillian Gatehouse
Emily Pulsford, BA

Illustrations
Mark Stacey p13 and 19

Designed and produced by
Atlantic Europe Publishing

Printed in China by
WKT Company Ltd

**Exploring the Maya empire
– Curriculum Visions
A CIP record for this book is available from the British Library.**

Paperback ISBN 978 1 78278 080 9

Picture credits
All photographs are from the Earthscape and ShutterStock Picture Libraries.

This product is manufactured from sustainable managed forests. For every tree cut down at least one more is planted.

The most famous Maya myth

Just like the ancient Greeks, the Maya had myths which were battles between heroes and evil, forces. The most famous myth from Maya times is called the Popol Vuh and it involves the struggle of twin heroes against the lords of the Underworld.

It all starts with the Hero Twins' father and uncle innocently playing ball near the Underworld. The lords of the Underworld are annoyed with the noise of the ball playing and two of them, One Death and Seven Death, send owls to lure the twins to the ballcourt of the Underworld.

The two men are captured and sacrificed by the lords of the Underworld and then buried in the ballcourt. The head of the Twins' father is hung in a fruit tree. The father's head spits into the hands of a passing goddess, who gives birth to the Hero Twins, Hunahpu and Xbalanque.

Once they are grown up, the Hero Twins find the ballgame equipment in their father's house and start playing. This again annoys the lords of the Underworld, who summon the Twins to play the ballgame. Here they have to overcome trials and dangers. During this match the bats cut off the head of Hunahpu. His brother uses a squash (fruit) as Hunahpu's head to carry on playing until his real one, which is being used as a ball by the lords, can be won back and fitted onto Hunahpu's body again.

The Twins then play the ballgame with the lords of the Underworld, defeating them. But not everything is well: the Twins cannot bring their father back to life, so they leave him buried in the ballcourt of the Underworld.